BEYOND THE
SPOTLIGHT

(A BIOGRAPHY)

AMANDA GERALDINE

TABLE OF CONTENTS

PREFACE

Born on the 1st of February, 1994, Harry Edward Styles is a multifaceted talent hailing from England. His journey into the world of music and acting started in 2010 when he became a vital part of the renowned boy band, One Direction. Interestingly, this group found its inception on the British music competition series, The X Factor, as each member, including Styles, had previously faced elimination as solo contestants. This twist of fate led to the formation of One Direction, which later soared to become one of the best-selling boy groups in history. Their rise was marked by a series of hits that captivated the hearts of fans worldwide. However, in 2016, the band decided to embark on an indefinite hiatus, leaving behind a trail of remarkable achievements.

Styles' solo musical odyssey took flight with the release of his eponymous debut album under

Columbia Records in 2017. The album made an astonishing debut, claiming the top spot on both the UK and US charts. Its standout single, "Sign of the Times," not only conquered the UK Singles Chart but also established Styles as a force to be reckoned with in the solo music scene.

The year 2019 saw the release of Styles' second album, "Fine Line," which made an even grander statement. The album dominated the US Billboard 200 chart, boasting the largest first-week sales by any English male artist up to that point. Adding to its laurels, "Fine Line" secured a coveted spot on Rolling Stone's prestigious "500 Greatest Albums of All Time" list in 2020. The infectious single "Watermelon Sugar" further solidified Styles' presence by reigning atop the US Billboard Hot 100.

Breaking new ground, Styles unveiled his third album, "Harry's House," in 2022. The album swiftly shattered records and garnered widespread acclaim, culminating in a Grammy Award for Album of the Year in 2023. The album's leading track, "As It Was," resonated globally and earned the distinction of becoming the foremost song of 2022 according to Billboard's rankings.

Recognized for his exceptional contributions, Styles has amassed an impressive array of accolades. Among these are six Brit Awards, three Grammy Awards, an Ivor Novello Award, and three American Music Awards. Impressively, his artistic prowess isn't confined to the realm of music, as he's also made a mark in cinema. Roles in notable films like "Dunkirk" (2017), "Don't Worry Darling" (2022), and "My Policeman" (2022) have showcased his versatile acting skills.

Beyond his artistic pursuits, Styles is celebrated for his distinctive and bold fashion choices. His daring and unique sense of style has captured attention, making him a trendsetter in the world of fashion. In a groundbreaking move, he made history by gracing the cover of Vogue magazine as the first solo male cover star.

All in all, the journey of Harry Styles is one marked by musical triumphs, acting achievements, and an undeniable influence on the fashion landscape. His evolution from a member of a boy band to a global solo sensation showcases not only his talent but also his ability to continually redefine the boundaries of his creative expression.

EARLY YEARS

In the early chapters of his life, Harry Edward Styles took his first breath on February 1, 1994, in the town of Redditch, Worcestershire, nestled within the English countryside. His parents, Anne Twist (née Selley), who owned a local establishment, and Desmond "Des" Styles, who toiled in the realm of finance, welcomed him into the world. As a child, his family relocated, encompassing him, his parents, and his older sister Gemma, to the serene village of Holmes Chapel in Cheshire, England.

Life held its own intricacies for young Styles. The tender age of seven saw his parents part ways, their paths diverging. In time, his mother, Anne, entered a new chapter by marrying her business partner, John Cox, only for their journey together to conclude in separation as well. It was in this intricate web of relationships that Styles found himself welcomed into the fold of Robin Twist's family, through Anne's marriage to him in 2013. The unfortunate sting of cancer claimed Robin Twist's life in 2017, leaving Styles with an older stepbrother, Mike, and a stepsister named Amy, from this union.

Styles often reminisced about his formative years with fondness, describing his childhood as something truly special. The unwavering support of his parents formed a cornerstone for his growth. From a young age, music coursed through his veins. A karaoke machine bestowed upon him by his grandfather became a vessel for his burgeoning talent. It was through this that he delivered his first recorded performance, a rendition of Elvis Presley's timeless melody, "The Girl of My Best Friend."

Educational pursuits led Styles to the corridors of Holmes Chapel Comprehensive School. His distinctive voice led him to the forefront of the band White Eskimo, a group that gained recognition by emerging victorious in a local Battle of the Bands competition. Notably, this marked the genesis of Styles' journey into the music world.

In his zest for life and a desire to contribute, Styles also took up a part-time role at the W. Mandeville Bakery in Holmes Chapel. This period of his life, teeming with youthful enthusiasm and a taste of the ordinary, would later serve as a testament to his grounded nature amidst the whirlwind of fame.

CAREER

THE X FACTOR AND ONE DIRECTION (2010–2015)

Upon the suggestion of his mother, a pivotal moment in Harry Styles' journey unfolded on April 11, 2010. He took a leap of faith and auditioned as a solo participant for the seventh season of the esteemed British singing competition, The X Factor. His rendition of Train's "Hey, Soul Sister" didn't quite resonate with Simon Cowell, who advised him to choose a different path. Subsequently, Styles belted out a heartfelt version of Stevie Wonder's "Isn't She Lovely," a choice that resonated better with the judges.

While his initial solo journey came to an end at the boot camp stage, destiny had more intricate plans in store. In a fascinating twist, Styles joined forces with four other contestants of his age group who had also been eliminated. This quintet, consisting of Styles, Niall Horan, Liam Payne, Louis Tomlinson, and Zayn Malik, was formed in July 2010 to compete in the "Groups" category under the mentorship of Simon Cowell. During their two weeks of intensive practice, it was Styles who coined the name "One Direction" for the ensemble, a moniker that his bandmates readily embraced. With their musical camaraderie and distinct energy, the group began to make waves in the UK music scene.

The swift rise of One Direction was marked by their emergence as Simon Cowell's last act standing in the competition's live shows. Captivating audiences across the United Kingdom, they progressed to the final stage of The X Factor, ultimately securing a third-place finish. This pivotal moment marked the beginning of a journey that would redefine pop music history.

In January 2011, One Direction inked a record deal with Syco Records, Simon Cowell's label. The year saw the release of their debut single, "What Makes You Beautiful," which swiftly claimed the number one spot on the UK charts. Their inaugural studio album, "Up All Night," also debuted, showcasing three songs co-written by Styles. In a groundbreaking achievement, the album propelled One Direction to the distinction of being the first British group to have their debut album reach number one in the United States.

The subsequent years witnessed a parade of successes for the group, as their albums "Take Me Home" (2012), "Midnight Memories" (2013), "Four" (2014), and "Made in the A.M." (2015) all debuted at number one in the UK charts. Notably, "Midnight Memories" earned the title of the world's best-selling album of 2013, setting the stage for their unparalleled musical impact. Their presence was further solidified by a series of chart-topping singles including "Live While We're Young," "Little Things," "Best Song Ever," "Story of My Life," "Drag Me Down," and "History."

Styles' creative prowess extended beyond his own group, as he co-wrote the song "Just a Little Bit of Your Heart" for Ariana Grande's 2014 album "My Everything." As One Direction's trajectory continued to ascend, Styles advocated for a conscious decision to avoid overexerting their loyal fan base. His recommendation prompted the group to embark on an indefinite hiatus in 2016, following the culmination of promotional activities for "Made in the A.M."

One Direction's impact on the music scene was undeniable, culminating in a staggering 70 million records sold worldwide. Their accomplishments were marked by numerous awards, including Brit Awards, American Music Awards, Billboard Music Awards, and MTV Video Music Awards. Despite the rosy exterior, Styles has candidly shared that the intense visibility of being in the limelight wasn't always a walk in the park. He disclosed the challenges he faced in dealing with constant scrutiny, leading to his cautious approach to social media and interviews. His journey also encompassed navigating contractual terms, including "cleanliness clauses" during his time with One Direction, which he later shed tears of relief over when signing a solo contract without these constraints.

In the tapestry of his life, Styles' time with One Direction was a chapter of immense growth and accomplishment, though it carried its own complexities. As he ventured into a new phase of his career as a solo artist, the lessons learned and the memories shared with his bandmates remain an integral part of his artistic evolution.

HARRY STYLES AND DUNKIRK
(2016–2018)

Embracing his solo journey, Harry Styles forged ahead, aligning himself with Jeffrey Azoff's Full Stop Management and the renowned talent agency CAA. A major milestone emerged when Styles inked a recording contract with Columbia Records during the initial half of 2016, paving the way for his independent musical path. Around the same period, he unveiled his own record label, Erskine Records, a move that showcased his intention to not only craft music but to shape a distinct artistic identity.

The genesis of Styles' debut album began in 2016, an intricate tapestry woven across multiple locales, including Los Angeles, London, and Port Antonio, Jamaica. The latter served as the backdrop for a two-month creative sojourn in the autumn, during which Styles and his collaborators engaged in an immersive writing retreat. This voyage set the stage for the creative exploration that would come to define his musical narrative.

In March 2017, the world stood on the brink of a new musical era as Styles announced the release of his maiden solo single, "Sign of the Times," with a release date set for April 7. This poignant song scaled the heights of the UK Singles Chart, securing the number one spot, while also asserting its presence on the Billboard Hot 100 at number four. The track, a blend of glam rock and soft rock power ballad, drew parallels to the legendary David Bowie's work and was celebrated by Rolling Stone as the best song of 2017.

The accompanying music video further etched Styles' unique artistic expression in the public consciousness, featuring him soaring through the skies and walking on water. Its excellence earned him the prestigious Brit Award for British Video of the Year. Styles' musical prowess transcended borders, as he graced the stage as a musical guest on Saturday Night Live in the US and showcased his debut televised solo performance on The Graham Norton Show in the UK.

May 2017 marked the grand unveiling of Styles' self-titled debut album, an opus that swiftly captured the hearts of audiences across the globe. Its entrancing blend of 1970s soft rock earned it accolades as a "classic cocktail of psychedelia, Britpop, and balladry." With the world at his feet, Styles embarked on his inaugural headlining concert tour, "Harry Styles: Live on Tour," spanning continents from North and South Americas to Europe, Asia, and Australia. The tour was a testament to his magnetic stage presence and the fervor of his fan base.

Styles' creative tapestry expanded beyond music, as he ventured into the world of cinema with his feature film debut in Christopher Nolan's epic war film "Dunkirk." His portrayal of British soldier Alex in the context of the Dunkirk evacuation during World War II drew praise for its authenticity and skill.

Television wasn't left untouched, as Styles starred in the BBC One special "Harry Styles at the BBC," a one-hour showcase presented by Nick Grimshaw. The Victoria's Secret Fashion Show in Shanghai beckoned Styles' performance, solidifying his presence in the global entertainment sphere. His remarkable achievements were acknowledged with the Best International Artist award at the 2017 ARIA Music Awards.

An array of creative endeavors marked Styles' journey, including co-writing "Alfie's Song (Not So Typical Love Song)" for the soundtrack of the film "Love, Simon," executive producing the CBS sitcom "Happy Together," and even entering the realm of fashion as a Gucci model. His evolution, far from a linear trajectory, was a mosaic of musical exploration, cinematic ventures, and cultural impact that cemented Styles as a true artistic chameleon.

FINE LINE (2019–2021)

In July 2019, a potential turn in Styles' journey emerged as reports surfaced that he was in preliminary discussions to portray Prince Eric in Disney's live-action adaptation of "The Little Mermaid." However, he eventually decided to decline the role due to a combination of factors, including his ongoing tour commitments and a desire to explore darker, non-musical roles. This pivotal role eventually found its home with Jonah Hauer-King.

Amidst this cinematic interlude, Styles continued to paint his musical narrative. His lead single from the second album, "Fine Line," titled "Lights Up," made its debut in October 2019, swiftly rising to the third position on the UK charts. The song marked a gentle re-entry into the pop realm, with its captivating melody and lyrical depth resonating with audiences.

Adding to his diverse repertoire, Styles assumed dual roles as both host and musical guest on the iconic television show "Saturday Night Live" in November, showcasing his versatility and captivating stage presence. December saw the release of "Adore You," the second single preceding his album "Fine Line." The song soared to the seventh spot on the UK charts and the sixth position on the US charts, solidifying Styles' enduring appeal.

On the 13th of December, "Fine Line," his sophomore album, was unveiled. Crafted at the Shangri-La studio in Malibu, California, it retained the signature sound of his debut while infusing elements of funk and soul, resulting in a dynamic musical experience. Critics lauded the album's blend of influences, and it made a profound impact on the charts, reaching the pinnacle in the US and securing the second spot in the UK.

"Fine Line" spawned an array of compelling singles, including "Falling," "Watermelon Sugar," "Golden," "Treat People with Kindness," and the titular track. The infectious "Watermelon Sugar" surged to the top of the charts, earning Styles his first number-one single in the US and his fourth UK top-ten single. Rolling Stone's esteemed "500 Greatest Albums of All Time" list included "Fine Line," solidifying its place in the pantheon of musical greatness.

Styles' tour in support of "Fine Line," named "Love On Tour," was initially scheduled for 2020 but faced postponement due to the global COVID-19 pandemic. The rescheduled tour was slated for 2021, a testament to his unwavering dedication to his fans and his craft.

Recognition and accolades continued to cascade upon Styles. At the 2020 Brit Awards, he secured nominations for British Male Solo Artist and British Album of the Year. He engaged in unique creative endeavors, performing an NPR Tiny Desk concert and narrating a soothing bedtime story titled "Dream with Me" for the relaxation app Calm.

Styles' collaborative efforts also extended to co-writing the song "Changes" for Cam's album "The Otherside." This spirit of collaboration bore fruit as he clinched awards at the 48th American Music Awards, the 34th ARIA Music Awards, and the 27th Billboard Music Awards. The title of Variety's Hitmaker of the Year bestowed upon him underscored his profound influence on the music industry.

In the sphere of cinema, Styles made an unexpected appearance in the Marvel Cinematic Universe film "Eternals," portraying Eros / Starfox, the brother of Thanos, in a mid-credits scene. In a unique stride, he ventured into the beauty realm, launching the gender-neutral skin and nail care brand, Pleasing.

As Styles continued to navigate the ever-evolving landscape of creativity, his diverse accomplishments showcased his multifaceted talents and a relentless pursuit of innovation.

HARRY'S HOUSE AND OTHER ROLES (2022—2023)

The year 2022 marked a crescendo in Styles' artistic journey, as he unfurled his third album, "Harry's House," to widespread acclaim. The album's lead single, "As It Was," made a monumental debut by claiming the top positions on both UK and US charts, achieving his second solo number one in both nations. In the US, the song's reign as number one endured for an impressive 15 weeks, making it the fourth-longest-running chart-topper in the country's history. The album itself mirrored this triumph by securing the number one spot on charts in both the UK and the US. Styles' dominance was indisputable during its release week, with "Harry's House" and "As It Was" jointly reigning at the summit of the album and singles charts in both countries. An extraordinary feat was achieved as four tracks from the album concurrently secured positions within the US top 10, marking Styles as the first British solo artist to attain this milestone. His music echoed through the exalted grounds of the Coachella Valley Music and Arts Festival, where he headlined in April, further solidifying his status as a global musical icon.

As June dawned, Styles' influence extended into the realm of technology, with a captivating AirPods commercial for Apple featuring his song "Music for a Sushi Restaurant." A visual masterpiece accompanied the release of the second single from "Harry's House," as the music video for "Late Night Talking" captured audiences' imagination in July.

The accolades continued to cascade, as "Harry's House" earned a coveted spot on the shortlist for the Mercury Prize, a distinction that underscored the album's exceptional impact. Recognition at the 2022 MTV Video Music Awards culminated in three accolades, with "Album of the Year" for "Harry's House" taking center stage. Styles' musical triumph extended to the grand stage of the Grammy Awards, where "Harry's House" clinched the titles of "Album of the Year" and "Best Pop Vocal Album." Across the Atlantic, the Brit Awards added another laurel, as "Harry's House" secured the honor of "British Album of the Year."

Styles' talents transcended the boundaries of music, as he auditioned for the role of Elvis Presley in Baz Luhrmann's musical biopic "Elvis." While recognized for his talent, Luhrmann noted that Styles' iconic status might present a challenge for portraying the legendary musician. On the silver screen, Styles' cinematic journey continued with his appearance alongside Florence Pugh in the psychological thriller "Don't Worry Darling," directed by Olivia Wilde. Premiering at the 79th Venice International Film Festival, the film garnered a mix of reviews, with Styles' performance receiving varied assessments. His role alongside Emma Corrin in "My Policeman," a film adaptation of a 2012 novel, premiered at the Toronto International Film Festival. While accolades were bestowed, reviews highlighted Styles' growth as a leading man in such complex narratives.

Styles' meteoric rise manifested in a historic moment at Madison Square Garden, where he performed 15 sold-out shows during his "Love On Tour." To honor this achievement, a permanent banner bearing his name was raised within the iconic venue, solidifying his status as the third musical artist in history to receive such recognition at the Garden. His partnership with Gucci continued to bear fruit, as the collaborative collection "Gucci Ha Ha Ha" was unveiled in November.

The year culminated with Styles reigning victorious at the American Music Awards of 2022, clinching titles as "Favorite Male Pop Artist" and "Favorite Pop Song." As the final notes of 2022 resonated,

Styles' journey remained an unceasing symphony of creative innovation, solidifying his status as an icon who continually pushes the boundaries of artistic excellence.

ARTISTRY

STYLE AND INFLUENCES

Styles' musical journey has been a captivating symphony of genres, weaving together elements of pop, pop rock, rock, soft rock, new wave, synth-pop, folk, and Britpop. His ability to seamlessly traverse these musical landscapes has resulted in a distinctive and ever-evolving sound that defies easy categorization.

The debut solo album that marked his foray into the spotlight was described as a "mish-mash of Los Angeles' style classic rock and ballads" by NME, evoking an "intimately emotional Seventies soft-rock vibe" according to Rolling Stone. Time magazine lauded the album for synthesizing influences from rock's expansive history, spanning decades. Styles' music showcases an innate ability to blend the essence of his musical inspirations into a unique sonic tapestry.

Influences that shaped his musical trajectory are wide-ranging, rooted in artists who have left an indelible mark on the music landscape. Artists like Pink Floyd, the Rolling Stones, the Beatles, and Fleetwood Mac have contributed to his musical foundation. The artistry of Harry Nilsson's songwriting, with its honesty and simplicity, has had a profound impact on Styles. His admiration for Nilsson's lyrical prowess speaks to a shared appreciation for raw and genuine expression.

Styles' second solo album, "Fine Line," was heralded for its evolution from his debut, seamlessly merging a nostalgic undertone with soaring pop sensibilities. This evolution mirrors Styles' philosophy of embracing change and growth, drawing inspiration from the fearless artistic journeys of icons like David Bowie and The Beatles.

Bowie, in particular, has served as a guiding light for Styles, with vintage clips of the legend serving as a source of inspiration and motivation during the creation of "Fine Line." His admiration extends to Freddie Mercury, Elvis Presley, and Paul McCartney, all of whom have left an indelible imprint on his musical sensibilities. Additionally, Shania Twain holds a special place in Styles' heart, not just musically but also as a fashion muse.

His musical influences also extend to albums that have left an enduring impact on him. "Astral Weeks" by Van Morrison and "At Last!" by Etta James are regarded as epitomes of musical perfection in his eyes. Even Pink Floyd's iconic "The Dark Side of the Moon" album, which he initially grappled with as a child, left an impression of musical sophistication that he found irresistibly cool.

Joni Mitchell's timeless masterpiece "Blue" struck a resonant chord, leading Styles to connect with one of the album's instrumentalists during the creation of "Fine Line." This amalgamation of influences, spanning eras and genres, reflects Styles' dedication to artistic growth, evolution, and a fearless spirit of musical exploration.

STAGE ACTS

As a solo artist, Styles has made a deliberate choice to take the stage as a rock artist, accompanied by a backing band that lends a powerful and dynamic live musical experience. In addition to showcasing his vocal prowess, Styles has embraced the role of an acoustic guitarist during his performances. His backing band has played an integral role in bringing his musical vision to life on stage.

Lead guitarist Mitch Rowland and drummer/vocalist Sarah Jones have been consistent members of Styles' touring ensemble, sharing the stage with him during his "Harry Styles: Live on Tour" and "Love on Tour" concerts. The band's composition has also included talented individuals like bassist/vocalist Elin Sandberg, pianist Niji Adeleye, percussionist and musical director Pauli Lovejoy, multi-instrumentalist/vocalist Ny Oh, bassist Adam Prendergast, pianist Yaffra, keyboardist/vocalist Claire Uchima, and guitarist/keyboardist/vocalist Charlotte Clark. This ensemble has contributed to creating an atmosphere that harks back to the rock festivals of the 1970s, as described by Jade Yamazaki Stewart of the Seattle Times.

Styles' stage presence and performance style have consistently left an indelible mark on critics and audiences alike. His energetic performances have been a hallmark of his shows since at least 2015, drawing comparisons to legendary figures like Freddie Mercury and Mick Jagger. Reviewing a One Direction concert in 2015, Rob Sheffield of Rolling Stone likened Styles' stage presence to Secretariat's iconic run, describing it as an exuberant display of love for the art of performance.

Styles' approach to performing has a unique athletic quality to it. He refrains from indulging in partying or substances after his shows, adopting a disciplined approach similar to that of an athlete. This dedication stems from his desire to deliver the best possible experience to his fans, viewing each performance as an opportunity to give his all.

In 2022, Craig McLean's portrayal of Styles' stage demeanor in The Face resonated with the sentiments of many. The review captured his on-stage persona as one of exuberant stomping and head-banging, a physicality that's both captivating and irresistible. Such dynamic performances have drawn comparisons to iconic figures in the rock realm, including the likes of Freddie Mercury, Mick Jagger, and Rod Stewart.

Through his dynamic live performances and undeniable charisma, Styles has carved a niche as a compelling and energetic rock performer, delivering shows that are as much about musical prowess as they are about creating a powerful connection with his audience.

PUBLIC PERSONA

Harry Styles has earned the titles of both a pop icon and a fashion icon, cementing his status as a multi-faceted artist. His journey from a boyband member to a successful solo artist has been met with praise and recognition for his exceptional talents and unique style. He's often regarded as one of the most successful solo artists to emerge from a band, deftly navigating a challenging transition that others before him, like Justin Timberlake and Robbie Williams, have also undertaken.

The influence of Styles' music has resonated far and wide. Stevie Nicks, the esteemed singer-songwriter, drew parallels between Styles' album "Fine Line" and Fleetwood Mac's iconic "Rumours," highlighting his creative impact. With his third album "Harry's House," Styles set a remarkable record for first-week vinyl sales, a testament to his immense popularity and enduring appeal.

Styles' impact goes beyond music and into the realm of fashion. His concerts have inspired a wave of creative attire from fans, often resembling a "Met

Gala" for his dedicated audience. This fashion movement has been showcased in prominent publications like Vogue, The New York Times, and The New Yorker.

The influence of Styles' persona has also extended into literature and film adaptations. Novels like the "After" series, "Grace and the Fever," and "The Idea of You" have been inspired by him. His immense following on social media platforms like Twitter and Instagram further solidify his status as a cultural influencer. On Spotify, he's one of the most-streamed artists of all time, with his song "As It Was" even claiming the title of the most-streamed song of 2022.

Styles' devoted fanbase, known as "Harries," reflects his widespread popularity. His immense online following has its drawbacks, however, with incidents of bottling and harassment affecting the artist during performances. Despite this, he remains one of the most-searched musicians on Google and is even the subject of an academic course at Texas State University, delving into his impact on celebrity culture.

While Styles' acclaim continues to grow, it's worth noting that such praise can sometimes stir controversy. The designation of him as the "new King of Pop" by Rolling Stone UK, for example, sparked criticism from fans and family members of Michael Jackson. These reactions highlight the complex interplay of recognition and comparison within the world of music and entertainment.

FASHION AND AESTHETICS

Throughout his career, Harry Styles' fashion evolution has been as dynamic and diverse as his musical journey. During his time in One Direction,

Styles made a striking fashion statement with his choice of wardrobe, which ranged from skinny jeans and sheer blouses to floral prints and flamboyant suits. His style transitioned from the teenage aesthetic of hoodies to a more sophisticated blend of '70s rock influences and a touch of glamorous flair. He often stood out as the "Class Clown," exuding charm and a sense of playfulness.

As the band matured, Styles began collaborating with stylist Harry Lambert, further refining his fashion sense. His appearance in Another Man magazine in 2016 marked a turning point, with observers recognizing him as an "artthrob" who embraced art and fashion over mainstream norms. His style during this phase was deemed more artful and niche, showcasing his allegiance to the world of art and fashion.

As a solo artist, Styles took his fashion choices to new heights. He embraced a colorful and flamboyant aesthetic, often seen in custom pink suits, sequined tops, and printed satin flares. His partnership with luxury brand Gucci became a hallmark of his style, and his fondness for the color pink even led him to declare it the "only true rock & roll color."

Styles' fashion choices were noted for their fun, fashion-forward, and theatrical qualities. His use of vibrant colors and bold patterns, along with his penchant for artful accessories, allowed him to tell stories through his outfits. His style drew comparisons to pop icons like the Spice Girls, reflecting a blend of theatricality and creativity in his fashion sense.

Harry Styles' fashion choices have not only been a reflection of his personal style but have also sparked discussions and pushed boundaries in the world of fashion and gender norms.

In 2019, Styles began sporting sweater vests, baggy high-waisted pants, and even pearl necklaces. His embrace of the manly pearl necklace led to him being called the "popularizer" of this trend. Some of Styles' fashion choices have contributed to discussions about gendered fashion, and his willingness to challenge traditional norms has been noted by critics and observers.

One of the most significant moments in Styles' fashion journey was when he appeared on the cover of Vogue in 2020, becoming the first man to do so solo. The cover featured him wearing a blue Gucci dress, which stirred both admiration and controversy. Right-wing commentators criticized his choice of attire, with some arguing that it challenged traditional notions of masculinity. Styles responded by emphasizing the importance of breaking down fashion boundaries and expressing oneself freely, regardless of gender norms.

His fashion choices haven't just been about breaking boundaries, but also about supporting small designers. For instance, the JW Anderson cardigan he wore during lockdown gained widespread attention and even prompted the designer to release the pattern for free online.

Styles' impact on fashion has been recognized by various awards and rankings, including winning the British Style Award at the Fashion Awards and being named GQ's "Most Stylish Man of the Year." He has been lauded for his embodiment of British rocker style and his ability to wear clothing with unapologetic swagger.

Overall, Styles' fashion journey has been marked by a willingness to challenge norms, spotlight emerging designers, and use his influence to spark important discussions about identity, gender, and self-expression in the world of fashion.

PERSONAL LIFE

Harry Styles' personal life reveals a mix of beliefs, routines, and values that shape his identity and actions.

Styles splits his time between different homes, including residences in North London, Manhattan, and Los Angeles. Despite previously living in LA, he became disillusioned with the city and sold his residence there. During the early days of his career, he lived in the attic of producer Ben Winston's home in London while he searched for his own house.

He holds spiritual beliefs and considers himself more spiritual than religious. Styles believes in karma and acknowledges the existence of forces beyond us. He practices pilates and meditation daily, as well as attending therapy regularly. His commitment to self-care and personal development is evident in his routines and practices.

In terms of his diet, Styles follows a pescatarian diet, abstaining from meat but including fish in his meals. He's also open about his health conditions, such as polythelia, which reflects his authenticity and transparency with his fans.

Styles' financial success is notable, as he consistently ranks highly on the Sunday Times Rich List of musicians under 30 in the UK. His estimated net worth has seen substantial growth over the years, and he has become one of the wealthiest young musicians in the UK.

Overall, Styles' personal life showcases a well-rounded individual who values his well-being, spirituality, authenticity, and financial success.

RELATIONSHIPS

Harry Styles' romantic relationships have garnered significant attention from the media and fans alike.

In 2011, Styles dated television presenter Caroline Flack, which attracted controversy due to their age difference, with Flack being 14 years older than him. This relationship sparked discussions about age dynamics and celebrity romance.

His brief relationship with American singer-songwriter Taylor Swift in 2012 added another layer of intrigue to his personal life. Their high-profile breakup led to speculation and fan theories about whether their songs were inspired by their time together.

From 2017 to 2018, Styles was romantically involved with French-American model Camille Rowe, who reportedly inspired his 2019 album "Fine Line."

This relationship added a personal touch to his music, as Rowe's influence was reflected in his creative work.

Styles' relationship with actress and director Olivia Wilde from January 2021 to November 2022 marked another chapter in his love life. Their relationship generated significant media coverage, showcasing the challenges of dating in the public eye.

Overall, Styles' romantic relationships have been closely followed by the media and fans, contributing to the narrative of his personal life and adding an additional layer of intrigue to his public image.

SEXUALITY

Harry Styles has faced persistent questions about his sexual orientation in interviews, a topic that has intrigued the public since he was 19 years old. The media has been curious about this aspect of his identity, leading to repeated inquiries and speculation. Styles, however, has consistently shown a firm stance on the matter, choosing not to define or label his sexuality publicly. This has been a topic of discussion in various interviews and articles throughout his career.

In a 2013 interview with British GQ, Styles was asked about being bisexual, to which he responded, "Bisexual? Me? I don't think so. I'm pretty sure I'm not." This initial response set the tone for his approach to questions about his sexual orientation. He continued to face such queries in subsequent interviews, often responding with a thoughtful and measured perspective. In a 2017 interview, Styles stated, "No, I've never felt the need to really. I don't feel like it's something I've ever felt like I have to explain about myself."

Styles' views on sexuality and identity became more elaborated in later interviews. In a 2019 interview with The Guardian, he tackled the issue of his flamboyant dressing style and perceived ambiguity. He clarified that his choice of attire wasn't about trying to project a certain sexual orientation; rather, it was a matter of personal expression and aesthetics. Styles emphasized his belief that sexuality is something fun and creative, not a rigid aspect that defines a person.

His perspective deepened in a 2022 interview with Better Homes and Gardens. Styles spoke candidly about his personal experiences and the shifting societal attitudes towards sexual orientation. He highlighted that he has been open about his sexuality with his friends, but he firmly believes that labeling oneself should not be obligatory. Styles asserted that the expectation for public figures to publicly label their sexual orientation is outdated and counterproductive. He stressed that the journey towards a more accepting and inclusive society involves moving away from labeling and categorizing, instead focusing on acceptance and embracing individual experiences.

In essence, Styles' approach to questions about his sexual orientation revolves around the idea that it's a personal aspect of his identity, one that he believes doesn't require a public label. His stance reflects the changing dynamics of discussions around sexuality and identity, emphasizing individuality and pushing back against societal expectations. Through his statements and interviews, Styles has contributed to a larger conversation about acceptance, authenticity, and the evolving nature of personal identity.

PHILANTHROPY AND ADVOCACY

Throughout his career, Harry Styles has been an advocate for various charitable causes and social issues, using his platform and influence to raise awareness and support meaningful initiatives.

In 2013, Styles and Liam Payne, his fellow One Direction member, became ambassadors for the cancer charity Trekstock. Together, they successfully raised over $800,000 through online fundraising for the organization. Styles' commitment to equal rights was evident when he responded to the Westboro Baptist Church's picketing of a One Direction concert in 2013. He took to Twitter to express his belief in equal rights for everyone.

Styles has consistently demonstrated his support for the LGBTQ+ community. He participated in

Stonewall's #FirstSnog campaign in 2014, celebrating the charity's 25th anniversary and promoting LGBT rights. During One Direction's concert in St. Louis, Styles wore the jersey of Michael Sam, the first openly gay player drafted by an NFL team, as a show of support. He often waves pride flags thrown on stage by fans and even assists fans with coming out publicly during his concerts, creating an atmosphere that many fans describe as a "safe space." His advocacy earned him recognition, including a Gay Times Honour for LGBTQ Advocate.

In addition to his LGBTQ+ advocacy, Styles has been involved in various charitable endeavors. He endorsed Emma Watson's HeForShe gender equality campaign in 2014 and sponsored water wells in India to support World Water Day. He donated his hair to the Little Princess Trust, an organization that provides wigs made of real hair to children with hair loss due to illness. He organized intimate shows in London and Los Angeles in 2017, with all proceeds benefiting charities. Styles also performed at events like CBS Radio's We Can Survive concert for breast cancer awareness.

Styles' tours have also served as platforms for charity initiatives. His first tour raised $1.2 million for 62 charities globally, while his second tour raised $1 million for organizations such as Physicians for Reproductive Health, Black Voters Matter, and Choose Love. These tours also promoted environmental causes by encouraging water conservation and reducing plastic bottle usage.

In 2018, Styles used his merchandise to support causes, selling T-shirts with the slogan "Treat People with Kindness" in rainbow print for Pride Month, with profits benefiting GLSEN. He also lent his voice to important social issues, tweeting in support of the March for Our Lives petition and displaying stickers on his guitar advocating for Black Lives Matter and an end to gun violence. Styles has identified as a feminist and has expressed his desire to find a cause that resonates with him personally, where he can dedicate his full support and make a significant impact.

In all these efforts, Styles has demonstrated a genuine commitment to social change and has used his influential position to contribute positively to the world around him.

Harry Styles has been acutely attuned to the political and social landscape, allowing his music and actions to reflect the pressing issues of the times. His song "Sign of the Times" is a poignant example of this approach. He acknowledged the impact of events like Brexit, the Black Lives Matter movement, and Donald Trump's presidency on his music, recognizing that we live in a world where global occurrences are impossible to ignore. Styles noted that it would have been odd not to acknowledge such significant events in his work.

Styles' political leanings are left-leaning, and he has engaged with political matters on multiple occasions. He demonstrated his interest in the political process when he visited the House of Lords in 2016 to attend a debate on Brexit. He expressed a viewpoint that prioritizes unity and togetherness, stating that anything that brings people together is preferable to things that create divisions. He openly opposed Brexit, viewing it as contrary to the type of world he envisions.

In response to the tragic killing of George Floyd in 2020 and the ensuing global outcry for racial justice, Styles demonstrated his support for the Black Lives Matter movement. He encouraged his fans to share and donate to the cause and pledged to contribute to a bail fund for arrested activists.

Styles took his activism to the streets by attending a Black Lives Matter protest in Los Angeles.

During the 2020 United States presidential election, Styles, despite not being a U.S. citizen, endorsed Joe Biden, indicating his alignment with certain political values and his willingness to use his voice to advocate for change.

In a demonstration of his commitment to humanitarian causes, Styles announced in June 2022 that he would donate his appearance fee from Apple's AirPods' spatial audio campaign to the International Rescue Committee. This organization is dedicated to providing aid to refugees who have been forced to flee Ukraine due to the conflict there.

Overall, Harry Styles has consistently demonstrated his engagement with pressing political and social issues, using his platform to raise awareness, support causes, and inspire positive change.

TREAT PEOPLE WITH KINDNESS

The phrase "Treat People with Kindness," often abbreviated as "TPWK," has become a central message and slogan championed by Harry Styles to spread a message of love, acceptance, and kindness to others. Styles introduced this slogan during his debut concert tour in 2017, where it appeared on a badge attached to his guitar strap and was featured on tour merchandise, including Pride T-shirts that were sold to raise funds for the GLSEN organization.

The impact of the TPWK initiative became evident as Styles noticed the growing popularity of the slogan. He mentioned seeing people wearing

TPWK T-shirts and felt that it had developed into something meaningful and recognizable. This inspired him to create a song named after the slogan, which became the penultimate track on his second studio album, "Fine Line."

In October 2019, fans around the world spotted teaser posters bearing the phrase "Do you know who you are?" and the acronym "TPWK" in major cities such as London, Tokyo, Los Angeles, New York, and Australia. The posters created excitement and anticipation among fans, who quickly linked them to Harry Styles and his upcoming album release due to the reference to his "Treat People with Kindness" motto.

Coinciding with World Mental Health Day, Styles launched a unique online initiative titled "Do You Know Who You Are?" The initiative featured a website bot that generated random positive messages for users, using words like "bright," "determined," "loving," and "wonderful." The messages concluded with "TPWK. LOVE, H," reinforcing the message of treating people with kindness and spreading love.

Overall, the TPWK slogan has not only become a recognizable symbol associated with Harry Styles but also a powerful message that encourages compassion and positivity, resonating with fans and promoting a culture of kindness.

MAHSA AMINI PROTESTS

In 2022, during one of his concerts, Harry Styles engaged with a powerful and relevant message brought forth by a fan's sign. The sign held by the fan read "STAND WITH THE WOMEN OF IRAN." In a striking moment, Styles took the sign from the fan and displayed it to the entire audience, amplifying the message and bringing attention to the important cause.

By showcasing this sign on stage, Styles used his platform to raise awareness about the struggles and challenges faced by women in Iran, a gesture that resonated with both the live audience and those who heard about it later. This action highlighted his willingness to support and bring attention to important social and human rights issues, further demonstrating his commitment to using his influence for positive change.

DISCOGRAPHY

Harry Styles' discography is a testament to his evolution as a musician. From his early days with One Direction to his successful solo career, his music has captivated audiences worldwide. His debut solo album, "Harry Styles," released in 2017, showcased his versatility with tracks like "Sign of the Times" and "Kiwi." The album's classic rock and folk influences set the stage for his distinct sound.

In 2019, Styles' second album, "Fine Line," revealed a more introspective and experimental side. Songs like "Adore You" and "Watermelon Sugar" became instant hits, blending pop sensibilities with his unique musical vision. The album's critical acclaim solidified Styles' status as a solo artist to watch.

Continuing his artistic journey, Styles released his third album, "Harry's House," in 2022. The album's lead single "As It Was" topped charts, showcasing his ability to fuse rock, pop, and soul seamlessly. With a musical maturity that belies his years, Styles' discography tells a story of growth, authenticity, and pushing creative boundaries.

Experience the evolution of Harry Styles through his music. From his debut to his latest release, his discography is a reflection of his artistry and passion. Dive into his world and discover the melodies that have resonated with millions. Explore his discography now and immerse yourself in the sonic journey of Harry Styles.

Printed in Great Britain
by Amazon

31803913R00036